Everyone needs
'A Little Black Book'.
A place to write 'secret
things' and to write 'stuff'
that you think about and
want to remember - and
not want to remember.
'A Little Black Book' is that
prized and treasured
notebook
that you keep close to your
heart.
The 'Little Black Book' that
takes you on journeys of
memories - and prepares
you for the next one.
Everything you need will be
in here.

Created especially for
you.....

Date: _______________________

Created especially for you

Date: _______________________

_______________________
_______________________
_______________________
_______________________
_______________________
_______________________
_______________________
_______________________
_______________________
_______________________
_______________________
_______________________
_______________________
_______________________
_______________________
_______________________
_______________________

Date: _______________

Created especially for you

Date: _______________________________

Created especially for you

Date: _______________________

Date: ______________________________

_______________________________________

Date: _______________________________

Created especially for you

Date: _______________________

Created especially for you

Date: ______________________________

Date: _______________________

Date: ______________________

*Created especially for you*

Date: ________________

Date: ________________________

Created especially for you

Date: _______________________________

Created especially for you

Date: _______________________

Date: _______________________________

Date: _______________________

_Created especially for you_

Date: ___________________________________

*Created especially for you*

Date: _______________________

Created especially for you

Date: _______________________________

Date: _______________________

Date: _______________

*Created especially for you*

Date: _______________________

Date: _______________________________

Created especially for you

Date: ______________________________

Created especially for you

Date: _______________________________

Created especially for you

Date: _______________________

*Created especially for you*

Date: _______________________

Created especially for you

Date: _______________________________

_______________________________________

_______________________________________

_______________________________________

_______________________________________

_______________________________________

_______________________________________

_______________________________________

_______________________________________

_______________________________________

_______________________________________

_______________________________________

_______________________________________

_______________________________________

_______________________________________

_______________________________________

*Created especially for you*

Date: ______________________________

*Created especially for you*

Date: ______________________

_Created especially for you_

Date: _______________________

Created especially for you

Date: _______________________________

Created especially for you

Date: ___________________________

Created especially for you

Date: ___________________________

Date: _______________________

_Created especially for you_

Date:

Date: ___________________________

Date: _______________________

Created especially for you

Date: _______________

*Created especially for you*

Date: ____________________________

Date: _______________________________

Date: _______________________

Date: _______________________

Created especially for you

Date:

Date: ___________________________________

Created especially for you

Date:

_Created especially for you_

Date: _______________________

Date: ___________________________

_Created especially for you_

Date: ______________________________

Date: ______________________________

*Created especially for you*

Date: ________________________________

Date: _______________________________

Date: _______________________________

Created especially for you

Date: _______________________________

Created especially for you

Date: ______________________________

Date: _______________________________

Created especially for you

Date: _______________________________

Date: _______________________

_Created especially for you_

Date: _______________________

Date: _______________________________

_______________________________________

_______________________________________

_______________________________________

_______________________________________

_______________________________________

_______________________________________

_______________________________________

_______________________________________

_______________________________________

_______________________________________

_______________________________________

_______________________________________

_______________________________________

_______________________________________

_______________________________________

_______________________________________

_______________________________________

*Created especially for you*

Date: _______________________

*Created especially for you*

Date: _______________________________

Created especially for you

Date: _______________________________

Date: ______________________________

Date: ___________________________________

_Created especially for you_

Date: _______________________

Date: _______________________

Created especially for you

Date:

Date: ______________________________

Created especially for you

Date: _______________________________

Date: _______________________

*Created especially for you*

Date: _______________________________

Created especially for you

Date: _______________________________

Date: _______________

Created especially for you

Date: ______________________

*Created especially for you*

Date: _______________________________

Date: ______________________________

*Created especially for you*

Date: ______________________________

Created especially for you

Date: _______________________________

_Created especially for you_

Date: ________________________________

*Created especially for you*

Date: _______________________________

Date: ___________________________

# Date:

Date: _______________________

Date: ________________________________

Date: ____________________

_Created especially for you_

Date:

Created especially for you

Date: ___________________

*Created especially for you*

Date: ______________________________

Date: _______________________________

Date: _______________________

Date: _______________________________

Date: _______________

_Created especially for you_

Date: _______________________

Date:

Date: _______________

Created especially for you

Date: ______________________________

Created especially for you

Date:

Date: ________________________________________

*Created especially for you*

Date: _______________

Created especially for you

Date:

Date: _______________________

Created especially for you

Date: ___________________________

*Created especially for you*

Date: _______________________________

Date: ______________________________

Date: _______________________________

*Created especially for you*

Date: _______________________________

<br>

Created especially for you

Date: _______________________

*Created especially for you*

Date: ___________________________

*Created especially for you*

Date: ________________________________

Created especially for you

Date: _______________________________

Date: _______________________

Date: _______________

*Created especially for you*

Date: ______________________

*Created especially for you*

Date: _______________________

Date: _______________________

_______________________________

_______________________________

_______________________________

_______________________________

_______________________________

_______________________________

_______________________________

_______________________________

_______________________________

_______________________________

_______________________________

_______________________________

_______________________________

_______________________________

_______________________________

_______________________________

_______________________________

Date: _______________________

# Date:

Date: _______________________________

Date: _______________________

Created especially for you

Date: _______________________________

_Created especially for you_

Date: _______________________

Created especially for you

Date: _______________________

*Created especially for you*

Date: _______________________

_Created especially for you_

Date: _______________________

Date: ______________________

Created especially for you

Date: _______________________

_Created especially for you_

Date: _______________________

*Created especially for you*

Date: _______________________________

*Created especially for you*

Date: _______________

*Created especially for you*

Date: _______________________________

_Created especially for you_

Date: _______________________

*Created especially for you*

Date: _______________________

*Created especially for you*

Date:

_Created especially for you_

Date: _______________________

Date: _______________

Date: _______________________

Date: _______________________

Date: ___________________________

Created especially for you

Date: ___________________

Date: _______________________

Date:

Created especially for you

Date: _______________________

Created especially for you

Date: _______________________

_Created especially for you_

Date: _______________

_Created especially for you_

Date: ______________________

*Created especially for you*

Date: _______________________________

*Created especially for you*

Date:

Date: _______________________

*Created especially for you*

Date: ______________________________

*Created especially for you*

Date: _______________________________________

_______________________________________

_______________________________________

_______________________________________

_______________________________________

_______________________________________

_______________________________________

_______________________________________

_______________________________________

_______________________________________

_______________________________________

_______________________________________

_______________________________________

_______________________________________

_______________________________________

_______________________________________

_______________________________________

_______________________________________

_______________________________________

*Created especially for you*

Date: _______________________________

Created especially for you

Date: _______________________________

Created especially for you

Date: ______________________________

_Created especially for you_

Date: _______________________________

Date: _______________________

_Created especially for you_

Date: ________________________________________

Created especially for you

Date: _______________________

Date: _______________________________

*Created especially for you*

Date:

Date: _______________________________

*Created especially for you*

Date: _______________________

Created especially for you

# Date:

*Created especially for you*

Date: _______________________

_Created especially for you_

Date: _______________________________

*Created especially for you*

Date: _______________________

*Created especially for you*

Date: _______________________

*Created especially for you*

Date: _______________

_Created especially for you_

Date: ______________________________

Created especially for you

Date: _______________________

*Created especially for you*

Date: ______________________

*Created especially for you*

Date:

_Created especially for you_

Date: _______________________

*Created especially for you*

Date: _______________________

Date: ___________

Date: _______________________

Created especially for you

Date: _______________________

Date:

Date: _______________________________

Created especially for you

Date: ______________

Date: _______________________

Date: _______________________________

*Created especially for you*

Date: _______________________

*Created especially for you*

Date: ___________________________

Created especially for you

Date: _______________________________

*Created especially for you*

Date: _______________________

*Created especially for you*

Date: ___________________________

Date: ____________________

Date: ___________________

_Created especially for you_

Date:

*Created especially for you*

Date: ______________________________

Created especially for you

Date: _______________________

Created especially for you

Date: ______________________________

www.ingramcontent.com/pod-product-compliance
Lightning Source LLC
Chambersburg PA
CBHW072220150726
48002CB00005B/1912